Pacific Pieces

poems by

Magdalena Louise Hirt

Finishing Line Press
Georgetown, Kentucky

Pacific Pieces

Copyright © 2024 by Magdalena Louise Hirt
ISBN 979-8-88838-497-8 First Edition
All rights reserved under International and Pan-American Copyright Conventions. No part of this book may be reproduced in any manner whatsoever without written permission from the publisher, except in the case of brief quotations embodied in critical articles and reviews.

Publisher: Leah Huete de Maines
Editor: Christen Kincaid
Cover Art: Magdalena Louise Hirt
Author Photo: Magdalena Louise Hirt
Cover Design: Elizabeth Maines McCleavy

Order online: www.finishinglinepress.com
also available on amazon.com

Author inquiries and mail orders:
Finishing Line Press
PO Box 1626
Georgetown, Kentucky 40324
USA

Puzzle Contents

Piece One—Break Open the Puzzle
        Poems from Guatemala to Panama... 1

Piece Two—Sort the Puzzle
        Poems within Panama.. 15

Piece Three—Building from the Corners
        Poems from Panama to the Galapagos 19

Piece Four—A Complicated Edge
        Poems within the Galapagos 33

Piece Five—Finish Images from Within
        Poems from a Pacific Crossing 37

Piece Six—Missing Piece & Completion
        A Poem from French Polynesia 67

For my Selkie Crew:

*Wee Rory, Spunky Mara, Gentle Lily, Adventurous T,
and my husband, the Captain that keeps us afloat, Nicholas.*

Piece One

Break Open the Puzzle

Poems from Guatemala to Panama

Goodbye Rio Dulce

Crocodile, fierce ant, giant spider
waiting in the muck, the leaf, the corner,

I see you. I nestled my babies within
you. Tarzan cliff, coffee plantation,

lava eruption, I feel you. River bend,
launcha boat, wild rooster, I hear

you. Cantaloupe, papaya, banana,
I taste you. Varnish, epoxy, downpour,

I smell you. Halyard pull, tipping,
Tijax, I experienced the whole you

like a well-tied knot for a hammock
that swings over a family of turtles.

Lights Off Belize

Motoring the inside of the reef
devouring the safety of rocks
to sleep under the stars, half-
moon, and ocean breeze.

Stilted cottages twinkle off
the make-shift, tin lean-to
homes where pineapples
and plantains fight flies.

Jungle reserves, dense
with life scurry with creatures
that hurry to work before
dawn, monkeys howling.

Full scuba tanks, prepped,
line the water edge. Ready
to keep life's rhythm inside
the lion fish, ceviche hunter.

My rhythm is slight bounce,
of the hull, motor-push,
current sway, dolphin play,
depth-watcher, lighthouse.

Upwind

or really
back
n'forth
in the
same
spot

Alone with Moon

She whispers stories on the wind,
and Gulf of Honduras calms,
puts the otherworld to sleep.

Wind stops, sails flutter, Moon
has silenced her audience.
Clouds clear from the North Star,

stories are better with tea and toast.
I lift my head through a hatch
to listen—this nowhere, nothing

is filled with so much suspense,
bottomless mystery, and eery
characters. The Moon's fingers

exaggerate the storytelling that fill
the craters of my soul like juicy
tidbits and a pristine, fulfilling end.

Stillness. Moonlight.

Things I am grateful for. The breeze

hovers around my shoulders—my own

sea scarf. Climbable swells—gently

bounce. A clear path—moon's gift.

360 degrees of stars—and clouds

with their seductive night moves.

A small smile creeps into the corners

of my lips—I know pre-dawn sea secrets.

I keep them within my aquamarine eyes.

No AIS

No Tri-colors. We sail dark
into the trail of the moon.
Honduras. Nicaragua. Both
known for piracy. With a plan,
bright lights, a machete,
an axe, a spear for fish, a flare
gun, kitchen knives, we will not
be victims. Scan the surface.
Scan again. Listen. Move
quietly. Distress call ready,
we speed perfectly through
the night with an exhilarating
wind. It's just these clouds.
They know something I don't.

Horrible. Miserable.

I crumble into a ball inside the thin
walkway of the galley with a burnt
meatball and small bowl of spaghetti
that I must stomach like the fear of men
that circle us in nine fishing boats.

Men that drive strong machines towards
us forcing us to fall off of our sail line
to avoid collision. Men that come close
and stay at a stalking distance. Desperate
men that need to take. I swallow a bite.

This fear is worse than a storm. Again,
I question, what have I gotten us into?

The swells build, the ocean is thinking
on us and wants to make it worse. Rory
loses it on me, then I lose it. Buckets filled,
hours of prep and cooking, regurgitated.

Horrible. Miserable. Burnt meatballs.
Children's puke on my pjs, again. Wrong
night to cook spaghetti. Hungry men
on the horizon. Face the fear. Stash
some knives, hide grandma's jewelry,
know the plan… Heel. Clutch. Sway.
Swing. Nicaraguan ledge hundreds
of miles from shore. Horrible. Miserable.

The Lily Constellation

Speeding at 8 knots in 20 knots, Lily
and I need wind in our faces not to puke.

We stare at the nine lights that appeared
on the water after sunset. Boats. Silence.

We choose to look up into the stars. There
we are not surrounded by desperation.

There wonder fills us in search. Venus,
Saturn, Jupiter aligned rise in the sky

like a doorway to a protected place,
a possibility of life with no violence.

I hear her giggle as we find Taurus,
Pleiades-escaping piracy possibility.

Saint Andrew Island
    ~Distant light on the horizon

Now, a squall is on us that blots out
the moon and stars. Soaring 10
knots in a 35 wind. Sails reefed.
Blasting through the darkness
off Nicaragua. Husband and wife
riding it in awe. It clears. He
sleeps. The stars pop for a moment.
Another squall. And another. I wish
I could lick them away like tasty cotton
candy at an amusement park. Sails bang.
Wind is funky. A small patch of sail
drags this 22 ton boat like a wetsuit
on a water slide. Poetry does
not suffice. Even if I dreamed
the best Poetry Speaks nerves,
audience, and thrill, I could
not make words for this trust
and plunge, blind faith
in instruments, and shipwright
hands. Sailing into darkness
is like the Saint you kiss hanging
on your neck to grant you luck.
Like the Saint on the mantle,
you build a fire for, a home
around. The Saint, you name
your child after to be protected
by unseen powers. The light
on the horizon that is hope.

Alone in the Dark

Leaning out into the night—
Sailing, soaring into darkness—
Wind tearing, grabbing at your soul—

Mother would not approve.

Middle School Dance

If you concentrate on her, she will
sway you back and forth—small, gentle,
subtle movements to the rhythm. She

cannot be persuaded to stop. She
knows the song better than you. Back
and forth, back and forth—a butterfly

with new wings—open and shut—to dry
the delicate extensions. She cannot stop—
even if you wanted to step away

before the dance was finished, she
would not unlock her hands joined
behind your neck—or her stare

that made your fingers on her hips
paralyzed. The phosphorescence
in the water—school disco light

spinning. The patch of stars peaking—
adult supervision. The love developing—
one that grips your heart so tight—

it may be hard to breath as you
let her rest her head on your chest
and become attached to her heartbeat.

Not Moving

In a Marina, tied secure.
To shower. To laundry.
For food. For wifi.
To breath.
We re-establish
ourselves.
But,
how strange
it is
to be
not moving.

Piece Two

Sort the Puzzle

Poems within Panama

Panama Transition

Night moves with our buddy boat,
Lucky Girl, Bocas to Shelter Bay.

Lights blink at each other. Company.
The darkness wobbles us. Motor on.

The unseen space that swallows
is less intimidating with friends.

The canal on the horizon puts
freighters about like lost, lonely

spiders. The new year brought
properly with fireworks, a countdown

Goonies. Rain sprinkles. Stars dwindle.
An invisible string holds two boats,

six kids, and four sailors as a constellation
holds together its stars. Virgo stands

strong on the horizon, unseen, behind
the rain clouds. The phosphorescent sea

twinkles brighter, warmer than the cold
expanse of space. It pours, cleansing

our salt and mud from Panama out.
Transitioning our moves—Pacific.

Splits Open

The sky
splits
open
with a river
of stars, and
the breeze
that follows
splits me open
on the ocean
—satisfied.

Piece Three

Building from the Corners

Poems from Panama to the Galapagos

Panama Canal

Harnessed.
Attentive.

We step the ladder up three flights
like we need a stepping stool
to reach an important hat stored
top shelf with a brisa weave, built
by hands, to connect to time, but
placed out of reach to tempt on.

Boarded.
Advised.

Guided through Gutan Lake. Feed
the crew. Coffee the crew. Pillow
and bed the crew. A strange sleepover
with the locals, line handlers, tying us to
the history, the work, the death, the life.

Step down.
Squeeze in.

Pacific in view. Atlantic remembered.
Three sailboats hold hands as the water
slips below slowly ushering the next step,
the next world, the next part of the circle.

Land divided.
Oceans connected.

What is Love?

Is it anchor up in the afternoon? An adventurous sail to the Galapagos? Is it waking wrapped in arms? Sentiments written on a card? A warm cake with plenty of frosting? Is it a warm stew in hand with a cool breeze? A hug from a friend? Perhaps it's being buried in the sand? Is it raising your dinghy for a long passage? Confronting disrespect with honesty? Is it laundry dried in the sun? Hoisting a sail? Catching a fish? A comforting voice on the radio? Is it the wind behind you? The moon above you? How about an erratic wave soaking you? Dinner conversation? Warm food? Could it be night cuddles from a child? A peaceful dream?

Then…

I've got it,
strapped in,
buckled and bound
to me
like a life jacket.

**Wind Against Tide:
Captain's Quarters**

Sometimes
you
make me
wanta jump ship.

Full Moon

For Michigan families, the February Moon is a frost moon
filled with cozy fires, shovels, iced cars, slippery roads,
when we start to count down, beg for Spring.

Here, night sailing, beneath Panama, we called it the Yeti Moon,
instead of howling like wolves, we yortaled like Yetis,
giggling and laughing, yortaling and giggling.

The silence in-between holds questions, what ifs.

Here, the moon is so bright, it's like a foggy day. The days
are intensely hot, shoulders beg for a break of shade.

Here, in the in-betweens, days are so sunny, it's hard to see,
see why? But then, the full moon sets as the sun rises, horizon
to horizon, partners, parents watching kindly and gently motivating
us to move forward like the growth of a tree ready to burst

with green life out the tips
of branches, like a fish after bait,
caught in the way of things.

Labyrinth

Endless. Far as I can see.

The puzzle of ghosts under

the moon, adrift. Water.

Water. More water. A compass.

A map. A motor. To escape.

Moon Thrown

His coveted night watch request
has been granted, my fifteen-year-old
son wakes me in the night, moon
brilliant, breeze perfect, Galapagos
birds resting on bow and aft, waves
and swells gentle. His time of watching
numbers and gages is passed to me.
He reports, a small gust where he
was prepared to let out the head sail,
then bring it back in, and the depth
finder pinging four feet then descending,
something visiting from the depths. We
giggle. Torch passed with a "Welcome
to the Night's Watch," and he returns
to his top bunk where his long, lanky
growing body has room to curl up next
to a hatch where the ocean whispers
into his dreams and sea spray wets
his appetite for night moves of a sailor.

Seabirds

Nine. From far off sea places. Oceans
away. Perch on us. Respite from sharks.
We sail. We motor. They rest. Squawk.
Under a full moon, they fly. Circling.
In the night, in the dark, one clips
its wing in the rigging near the spreader.
It flips back and forth with the waves.
No way to help it down in the night
at sea. The wind whistles. Storms cluster.
So close to the Galapagos. We can smell
the land in the air. The dead bird swings
back and forth. Was there something
we missed? Did we not name them?
Love them? Moral drops. Silence. We
listen more. Too much wind arrives.

Ghost Ship

comes on the line of a squall.
Dangerously close with so much
ocean. Hold your line. I'll hold mine.
Straight off the bow. We are bound
to collide. I change course. Veer
off. The vessel, Black Moon, is always
off my bow. AIS says a ship to port,
yet there's a light to starboard bow
and a squall to port that just won't
close the last two miles to reach me.
Surrounded. Balanced between.
Squeezed by mystery and space.

Free Bird

We climbed the mast
in high seas
to.
free.
the.
bird.

I suddenly feel lonely, but
the new birds that visited and fled
are coming in flocks. The water
and wind plays a sad music
that I enjoy. Not much longer.

0 Degrees 0.000

North to South. Just like that.
A second. A countdown anticipated,
but covered with a small disagreement,
a camera turned the wrong way, and
it's done. Like life. I kiss a rock, toss
it down to Neptune. Kerplunk. I imagine
it still sinking even now, slowly down
thousands of water feet deep into
the darkness passing, perhaps knocking
into giant water creatures trying to sleep.
My eldest son throws many more with
whispers. Just North of the Galapagos,
but officially, South. We were, we are,
sailing a close reach, fast, into the wind.
Sails stretch to their limits, fluttering,
vibrating with the speed of the Southern
Hemisphere. I must forgive myself,
be kind to my soul. Moments slip
like the surface past me. Look back?
Think forward? That's silly. Just now.
This second. In this now. I will be.

Sunrise Over the Galapagos

The Booby birds, with their colorful feet,
cling to the bow, webbed, ready. I stretch
my bare feet out in the cockpit to support
the bounce of the surface that makes me
contemplate to and fro, in the distance,
in the now: Isla San Cristobal, whalers,
scientists, tortoises, dragons, and selkies.

Piece Four

A Complicated Edge

Poems within the Galapagos

Covid

Like the rapid rivers of The Black
Jaws in *The Testament of Gideon
Mack*, I've fallen, rode the riptide,
broken my soul on the rocks, and am
sharing drinks with the Devil. He's put
the fever of fire in my lungs, my throat,
and stollen my voice. Whiskey's taste
is lost on me, joy in place is lost on me,
living after death is the state given
in return—after survival. Meanwhile,
in the cave of my boat, bobbing,
rocking, quarantined, I'll talk with him,
and, perhaps, figure out about the mess,
figure out which view is in my window,
or if I'll choose to open the hatch.

49 Feet

The world makes me sad.

Flooding, famine, environmental crisis,
and Russia invades Ukraine?! I wander
the streets by myself, looking. Couples,
whole families, no masks, touching
handles, menus, chairs, touching
their faces like a pandemic hasn't killed
hundreds of thousands of others, of us.

As a species, the light is off. I think
on Greta, so small, taking on the world,
eyes so open, she can't look away.
In a state, confused. Why isn't everyone
screaming? My insides turn, I pull
myself over to the side vomit rising,
taste of absolute nothingness engulfs
my tongue. A stranger looks me up
then down, disgust. I'm here too.
I'm. Not. Screaming. Silence. A taxi.
Back to 49 feet floating. The only part
of me that makes sense, rocks impatiently.

Piece Five

Finish Images from Within

Poems from a Pacific Crossing

Again

Taste of Covid lingers in my throat
and we leave behind land and disease,
war and confusion, for the open ocean
again. I watch the orange orb of an almost
full moon set with my son as we change
shifts, and most of the water is black
like the night, except, for the waves
we make. Bouncing on the surface,
full sail, in a near perfect breeze, water
ripples away from the hull, clearing
a path with bright, glowing phosphorescence
peeling a magic from below. My cough
interrupts my thoughts, some pain
remains from land to remind me, I was there,
again. But now, Venus, the Milky Way,
my son's sign, Virgo, fill me, and I know
the life we've chosen outside, surrounded
by wind and water is the right choice,
again. Weaving around, in-between,
below the isles of the Galapagos, I know
the four-hundred feet is filled with sharks.
I swam with them at Kicker Rock, between
the cliffs, in crevices, with one way in,
only the same way out. Hammerheads,
black-tips, white-tips, Galapagos sharks
passed under my fins like shadows. Turtles
hovered, cliffside, munching off the walls.
Sea lions floated upside down like children.
Blue-footed boobies, frigates nested.
Manta rays swam past at my level to say,
it was okay I was there. Land. Wasn't
so bad, as long as it contained me,
in the water, along side it. The breeze
feels thick with salt, moist with ocean,
but the pain in my chest, in my lungs,
reminds me that there, on land, some
plan has gone wrong. I spread my wings,
open my sails, Pacific is calling. Time
for me to be searching, a seabird, again.

Leprechaun Trickery

In the night, we've been turned around.
Our captain was heading us southeast.
Our son has led us back north.
I wake and point us west! West!
Instruments contradict. Wind disappears.
Other boats drift by. We are caught
in a St Patrick's vortex. It pours. It squalls.
Circles. Circles. West. Just hold the line.
Bob. Wait. Small children wake with sleepy
eyes to gifts from leprechauns, so why
do we turn in circles? I accept our fate.
Caught under the Galapagos. Never
to escape the grasp of sharks
and sea lions that must be pulling us back.
My daughter shouts, "Rainbow!" And just
like that, twelve knots of wind push us
at a racing four knots! It seems so fast.
We are grateful and thank the fairies
for letting us approach the pot o'gold,
forever, just out of reach, in the ocean.

The "Right" Direction

is difficult
when
there's
so much
blue

This or that, a few degrees, with this much distance, points you towards different countries: the Pacific isles jut out of the water welcoming calm starry nights in the Marquesas, or the North Pacific, American honeymoon, Honolulu, with beaches, promises, sunburns, and surfers. South. North. A few degrees. So much blue. So many decisions have brought me here.

Water everywhere.
Me.
Us. Nowhere.

Scorpius

Tonight, the full moon gives a spotlight
on our motor south. The trade winds
need to be reached, or we will run out
of food and fuel. Scorpius is on my mind.
Looming with its giant sting, a patient
evil, an entry to the underworld. Very
patient and quiet, it waits. Antares,
the red supergiant star of a heart,
pulsing, making it breathe, brings
life into death. Like this life, this
labyrinth of water, when even we know
the works of its currents and winds,
its patience, its nothingness, its otherworld
can sting us with quiet, deadly possibilities
that no one would hear, no one would see.
But tonight, it's gentle with us, patient,
letting us pass, get south. The sun rises,
rival to the moon, staring her down,
making her set, and our bananas,
carrots, and cantaloupe start to rot.

South

The trade winds! Engine off. Ahh.
Wind pours gently like a warm
bath, also as comforting as a dry
towel wrapped around me. Pulling
it in tight, soft. It's like the night sky
knows this by giving me a fluffy
cloud covering. The moon shines
with aura. It feels like a bright pin
to decorate my hair. The dark blue water,
my dress. Clothed by Earth's elements,
I am ready for a date. No shoes required.

Gravity. Huge Swells.

I'm so
fucking
tired.

Moon Attraction

Tonight, in the cockpit, alone, I lay
down to see you perfectly above me
shining through the hatch. The swells
move you in sight, out of sight, peeking,
teasing. I want to climb the wind to you,
share your view. Gravity keeps me,
strongly. Surface tension throws me,
plays with me. Maybe, this ocean,
the Pacific, is vast enough, to give me
time to finally figure it all, my adventure,
my purpose, my reason, my attraction.

Breathing

Before the moon rises, I strap
my youngest two's life jackets

to clamps, and before bedtime,
they lean over high side, out

above the waves, the trades push,
the swells knock us around, but

the stars,
the stars,

spread across the darkness as if
yelling at my children, look, look,

see—the meaning of life, the mystery,
them, with me, moving in this moment.

The Momma

Crew, Dad and Son, have let
the Momma sleep. At 4:30 am,
I rise on my own to my son
trimming the sails for me
and making the lines nice.
It's funny, the age, the switch,
when a child starts to dote
on a parent, like I haven't
been doing this since before
he existed. But, it's nice though
like I'm a delicate tulip needing
tending, assistance. He double
checks my life jacket is on
and disappears. The night is
a misty grey hiding the moon
but revealing the light. The Momma
bobs in the cockpit, wind behind,
waves to port side, and I remember
nights on Lake Michigan, never alone,
under a moon, surrounded by excited
family, taking a pleasure cruise before
tucking into bed. Where tulips line
the streets in spring and turn a misty gray
in darkness of night. Here, it is day nine,
distance, forward motion important.
Here, I sit alone, wondering on my son's
dreams, taking care of myself for him,
keeping my stem strong, so my petals
will attract the wind and water needed.

Magnets

A voice and cheer upon returned,
our buddy boat, lost day two, is heard
on SSB day nine in the vastness
of the Pacific. Four miles southeast,
we turn sharp to port soaring through
the waves, and within a half hour,
like magnets, as the sunsets vibrant
orange, their light is on the horizon.
The Milky Way trails the night sky,
the green twinkle of their starboard
light reminds me of magic, a mossy
glen in Ireland, a Scottish loch
in the Highlands, a toasty marshmallow
by an island beach fire, a friend's
hands ready to catch a line, a tight
hug when souls breathe, feet dangling
off a dock immersed gently in water,
a look of connection across nautical
miles, location, place, our movement
in wind synchronized, attracted,
enchanted, brought back together.

Cobalt Blue

Sunset. Sunrise. The ocean turns
a reflective steal, almost deep violet,
that we call cobalt blue. It is our favorite
hew. The water breaks with marshmallow
froth, looks like a pair of ripped blue jeans
I could slip on. The deep blue of a salty,
weathered sailor's eyes. The sky lightens
to a burnt fossil white. The ocean's vast surface
reminds me of an ivory, cratered moon, and I
am nested in the normal of an endless sail.

Never What's Expected

The moon rises, laughing, a huge smile,
baring a mouth full of teeth. It's not
what I expected. They said, Coconut
Milk Trail—easy, downwind, following seas.
It is, broad reach, waves to port, endless
current. Not as expected, it shoots us
over, through, across the Pacific, twice
as fast—as expected. Radar clicks clean.
No squalls. The stars say, "You're welcome,"
and fill every dark space available. Above,
the Southern Cross stays pointing to port
as we sail west. Polaris, Orion, my northern
friends for so many years, are gone. This,
perhaps was to be expected. Fantasy,
myths, place, fill my imagination, and I
am in the middle of nowhere—just fine.

Life Jacket Pillow

…and I
am greedy
for even
more
stars

I Lied

The waves are too big—
The wind won't keep us above—
The sunshine makes no difference—
Pep talks are annoying—
Even when we make the mid-way mark—
Beauty is too extreme—
Vulnerability is too unpredictable—
I lied—
It's terrifying.

…and so

the day sails on
with noises
of happy children
a comfortably
sleeping husband
and me
quietly
containing
possible
doom

Sea State. Mind State.

I am
an unreliable reflection
of my
unpredictable environment.

…and just like that

the ocean
sits
calm
like
the darkness
of the moon
the side
that always
sleeps

Dracula's Sunrise

The sun shares the sky
with the night. He lets
the moon keep her smile,
the stars keep watch,
and adds a perfect pink
line to the horizon
that gives the black
water a deep red hew.
An ocean of blood,
a seductive dance,
a stare I cannot break,
an invitation when I
have already arrived,
a watery waltz that I
choose never to stop.

Sound Waves

Whistle, slosh, womp, creak, whistle, sloosh, stretch, pull, the darkness so thick, sounds are my only company. Whistle, whistle, a creature of the ocean black could be so near. Womp, creak, pull, the wind and waves take me into nothing, nowhere, one direction. Further, sloosh, shhh, quiet. The ocean is in control—whistle, sploosh, pull.

The Point

Venus and the crescent moon
in the endless colors of sunrise.

My eldest daughter, Lily, rising
with the sun commenting on clouds.

My youngest, Rory, my sunrise kid,
sleepy-eyed, stumbling, looking for me.

The endless ocean, the hews of blue
she gives, our water world realized.

The wind, not only on my skin, filling
sails, but the invisible, invincible power.

Conversations in the cockpit that plan
life, change course, fill souls with laughter.

The galley challenges—stovetop swinging,
knives sliding, enough food for a month.

Sleepy cuddles, following sea, family
within reach, moments, stargazing.

Our home, movable, floating, exploring,
coming with us, the world—comfortable.

The point? What's the point? Being now.
Living as the earth lives—in movement.

In the Night

anything can happen. A womp
in my ear, like a whisper alarm,
and I'm up. Captain shuffles
from the cockpit, deck light,
"We've lost the Code Zero."

Our giant, purple spinnaker
flaps in the night, lines loose.
Life jackets, oldest son, pull!
Drop it! It's in the water! Pull!
On deck, a mess, it's saved.

Pole up, head sail out, main
to starboard, wing to wing,
new night plan. We tend
to lines in the cockpit, I send
the boys back to bed. Stars.

In the night, the small sounds,
the small moments, matter. Life
is in the womp. Survival needs
a family in tune with the wind.
In the night, lines snap—we won't.

Back Breaker—First Mate Useless

Like a spine twisted with life,
like an overused halyard that snaps,
a soft shackle that cannot hold,
I am a mom set aside, useless to help,
our Code Zero flaps in the wind,
poles hold sails that bang against
the mast, cleats start to loosen their hold,
and my back has known too much.

Lost at Sea

In the beginning, there is worry
of food, weather, a counting of days,
then, somewhere in between, days
and wind with water, the thirst
for land disappears, a seaworthy
sailor doesn't mind the endlessness
of crossing. You find yourself quietly
whispering, may it never end, may
our world just be this. The sea holds
you, takes you from all of it, gives you
what matters. Lost in the way of it.

Day In, Day Out

When the sun blares through
the hatches, when the wind slows
down to a nudge, when the sea
still toys with your balance, when
time is repetitively similar,
when you may, perhaps, be on
the same waters that you were before,
when the day of the week and date
of the month mean absolutely nothing,
when you catch yourself staring
into the vastness unmovable
with, perhaps, a meditative state,
you will find my arm swaying, me waving.

Waves

Lip, lap, and lick—
gentle, hungry little
droplets, spending
their time thinking
on me. Lip, lap, lick,
I must taste good.
The ocean cooks
me slowly. Stir, taste,
mmm, good. Lip,
lap, lick—soaking me
just enough till I'm
sweet, tender, el dente.
A flavor of wind, a spice
of sun—a dark blue
stew. Lip, lap, lick—
tasty as a sunrise.

So Close

Pacific songs fill
the ocean air,
further horizons
call us, ancestors
reach out a hand
to lift us forward,
we sail on and on
I peer over your shoulder,
learning by mimicking,
hands over your hands
as they steer the helm,
anchor chain links counted
a grasp in the sandy depth,
foundation, home with a hook.

It's not still

There—the numbness—still pulling moving
as far as the eye sees—a pulling venting,
pushing, stretching—the horizon.
Unreachable. Slanted, swaying within
a grasp. Remember it? Unattainable. It's
not about me—the lingering. It belongs
to the strange, the place, the uncanny,
the mileage, just numbers, ticking, moving,
breathing, upwards in liquid transition.

Mystical

Magical. Fantasy. Does not,
cannot define the cliffs protruding,
building, breathing, living in nowhere,
endlessness of nowhere, nothing,
waves beyond waves, only wind,
nowhere, nothing, limitless gift
of the ocean, the forestry, mountains,
miniature beaches, small safe fingers
of anchorage. Nope. Fantasy made real
does not begin to cover the magic mirage
that grants feet the privilege of land.

Piece Six

Missing Piece & Completion

A Poem from French Polynesia

Marquesas

Boulders, bubbles, build with names—
Nuku-Hive, Oa-Pou, Hiva-Oa, Taiohae
that fall hundreds of feet gently into
brilliant blue waters exploding on rocks
up into perfect pink skies, teaming trees.
Men of fish thrive with tons of tattoos,
beating themselves like drums, welcoming
women with flower headdresses, beads,
horses. The dark sand beaches spill forth
taunt children raised on mango trees,
two thousand a season, galloping mares,
colts, back and forth in spinning waves.
Anchors of strangers come and go, who
ink themselves permanently to remember
the voyage here, the dancing, the drums.
The middle of nowhere is the center
of everywhere. Life begins and ends here.
Sailors merely dip toes in the beginnings
attempting to achieve, or hold, the energy.

Magdalena Louise Hirt has a Master of Arts in English Literature from the University of Toledo and a Master of Letters from the University of Highlands and Islands for Scottish Highland and Islands Literature.

Magdalena has multiple published articles in *Cruising World*, one in *Enchanted Living*, and another in *Literary Traveler*. Her first two poetry chapbooks, *Levels of the Ocean* and *Her Sea-filled Arms: Layers of Blue* are available for purchase. Two more chapbooks, *Pacific Prescription: Leukemia Cyclone* and *Her Bloody Project* are due to be released in 2024, and her first book (with poetry and prose), called *Distant Story Blue*, will be released by 2025 She has four self-published chapbooks, an article published via E-book from being a featured speaker at a conference in Oxford, and poems that have been published in *The Holland Sentinel, News from Hope College, The Mill* from the University of Toledo, and on display at the Toledo Museum of Art, which included first place and finalist awards. At Grand Valley State University, she received 1st place in fiction and 2nd place in poetry for the Oldenburg Writing Contest. She has been a featured speaker at a literary conference in Boston and two Poetry Speaks at the University of Toledo. She is currently finishing a script, a novel, two more chapbooks, and a collection of short stories. With her teaching degree, she has taught Middle School Language Arts and Freshman Composition at the University of Toledo.

Currently, she homeschools her four children and writes from her sailboat, which is a Westerly 49, named *Selkie*. Their family of six sails to circumnavigate the globe. So far, they have cruised, wintered, and been through lockdown in the following locations: the Great Lakes of Michigan, the Caribbean, the Bahamas, Bermuda, Azores, Ireland, Scotland, Norway, the circle of the Baltic Sea, the Bay of Biscay, Canary Isles, Cape Verde, back to the Caribbean, the Dominican Republic, Guatemala, Panama, French Polynesia, the Kingdom of Tonga, and New Zealand. These locations completed an Atlantic circumnavigation and a Pacific crossing. Her family plans to finish a global circumnavigation by 2025 and continue to sail.

Magdalena enjoys cooking and dancing—most of the time together. With pen, spatula, and helm in hand, her sailing soul belongs on the sea where she chooses words, academics, ingredients, and destinations. Follow their story at www.sealongingselkie.net.

www.ingramcontent.com/pod-product-compliance
Lightning Source LLC
Chambersburg PA
CBHW020340170426
43200CB00006B/449